BEST AUSTRALIAN
POLITICAL CARTOONS
2023

Russ Radcliffe created the annual Best Australian Political Cartoons series in 2003. His other books include: *Man of Steel: a cartoon history of the Howard years* in 2007; *Dirt Files: a decade of Australian political cartoons* in 2013; and *My Brilliant Career: Malcolm Turnbull, a political life in cartoons* in 2016.

Russ has edited collections from some of Australia's finest political cartoonists, including Matt Golding, Judy Horacek, Bill Leak, Alan Moir, Bruce Petty, John Spooner, and David Rowe, and curated several exhibitions including *Moments of Truth*, *Dirt Files*, and *Suppositories of Wisdom*.

In 2013 Russ was awarded the Australian Cartoonists Association's Jim Russell Award for his contribution to Australian cartooning.

For the lovely Jossie

BEST AUSTRALIAN
POLITICAL CARTOONS
2023

NOT ALL
IT'S CRACKED UP
TO BE

AHEAD

edited by
Russ Radcliffe

SCRIBE
Melbourne • London

Scribe Publications
18–20 Edward St, Brunswick, Victoria 3056, Australia
2 John St, Clerkenwell, London, WC1N 2ES, United Kingdom
3754 Pleasant Ave, Suite 100, Minneapolis, Minnesota 55409, USA

Published by Scribe 2023

Copyright © this selection & introduction — Russ Radcliffe 2023
Copyright © individual cartoons — contributing cartoonists

All rights reserved. Without limiting the rights under copyright reserved above, no part of this publication may be reproduced, stored in or introduced into a retrieval system, or transmitted, in any form or by any means (electronic, mechanical, photocopying, recording or otherwise) without the prior written permission of the publishers of this book.

Cover, front: Matt Golding, *The Age*
Cover, back: Andrew Dyson, *The Age*
Title page: Reg Lynch, *The Sun-Herald*

Printed and bound in Australia by Ligare Book Printers

Scribe is committed to the sustainable use of natural resources and the use of paper products made responsibly from those resources.

Scribe acknowledges Australia's First Nations peoples as the traditional owners and custodians of this country, and we pay our respects to their elders, past and present.

978 1 761380 58 7

A catalogue record for this book is available from the National Library of Australia.

scribepublications.com.au
scribepublications.co.uk
scribepublications.com

cartoonists

Dean Alston	11, 97, 103, 107, 123, 131, 149, 185
Badiucao	141, 154, 155, 159, 161
Matt Bissett-Johnson	25, 41, 53, 174
Peter Broelman	12, 18, 48, 52, 62, 66, 153, 161
Warren Brown	179
Mark David	23, 55, 135
Christopher Downes	100, 107, 176
Andrew Dyson	20, 32, 44, 110, 147, 151, 159, 169, 179
John Farmer	14, 21, 43, 57, 105, 111, 113, 142
First Dog on the Moon	16, 47, 83, 85, 91, 99, 105, 135, 183
Matt Golding	4, 6, 21, 27, 35, 42, 57, 68, 72, 76, 89, 98, 109, 121, 126, 128, 144, 150, 178, 181
Megan Herbert	12, 23, 75, 83, 101
Judy Horacek	80, 81
Fiona Katauskas	vi, 6, 39, 43, 59, 69, 70, 71, 73, 79, 114, 120
Mark Knight	22, 25, 27, 51, 65, 101, 109, 117, 125, 140, 153, 185
Jon Kudelka	9, 10, 13, 36, 45, 78, 79, 82, 87, 95, 98, 104, 121, 133, 135
Sean Leahy	36, 100, 105, 119, 133, 167
Johannes Leak	51, 69, 75, 93, 108, 117
Glen Le Lievre	18, 29, 31, 40, 63, 73, 88, 94, 102, 112, 132, 145, 156, 162, 167
Brett Lethbridge	31, 35, 52, 62 87, 96, 111, 123
Reg Lynch	2, 17, 33, 49, 66, 184
Alan Moir	14, 17, 49, 55, 129, 137, 142, 146, 163, 173, 174, 181
David Pope	24, 29, 30, 38, 41, 45, 46, 50, 56, 58, 61, 65, 83, 84, 90, 115, 122, 125, 127, 130, 139, 144, 149, 151, 168, 171, 173, 182
David Rowe	15, 19, 28, 34, 54, 60, 86, 116, 118, 124, 127, 136, 138, 143, 148, 152, 157, 158, 160, 164, 170, 180, 186
John Shakespeare	11, 119, 129
John Spooner	89, 92, 155, 165, 176
Andrew Weldon	7, 74, 77, 97, 106, 145
Cathy Wilcox	8, 26, 37, 59, 61, 64, 67, 71, 77, 95, 103, 113, 114, 131, 134, 139, 141, 165, 166, 171, 172, 175, 177

Fiona Katauskas, *Echidna*

'A Yes vote in this referendum is a chance for all of us ... to be counted and to be heard on the right side of history.'
— Anthony Albanese

'We shall overcome because the arc of the moral universe is long, but it bends toward justice.'
— Martin Luther King Jr, 1968

'There are tranquil ages, which seem to contain that which will last forever, and which feel themselves to be final. And there are ages of change which see upheavals that ... appear to go to the roots of humanity itself.'
— Karl Jaspers, 1953

'We are on a stormy sea, without a shore. The shore is so far away, so unknown that our lives and perhaps the lives of those who follow will pass before we set foot and settle on it.'
— Alexis de Tocqueville, 1848

no one left behind

No one left behind. No one held back. How could you argue with Labor's appeal to the fundamental generosity of Australians: a helping hand for the struggling, without frightening the aspirational. Everyone's a winner! Anodyne, inoffensive, small target, maybe, but also reassuring — not quite 'relaxed and comfortable', but pretty close. It's the principle that Anthony Albanese took to the election, winning a famous victory, and the lights by which he intends to govern (p. 94).

After nearly a decade or so of ego-driven revolving-door leadership characterised by a paucity of policy ambition, climate obstructionism, top-down class warfare, fear-driven khaki rhetoric, and constant charges of dodgy dealing — oh yes, and a pandemic — it was a relief to have what appears to be a quietly competent technocratic government. As Paul Keating said, change the government, change the country. We're not at the change the country bit yet, but the tone and atmospherics are different.

Albanese believes Labor should be the natural party of government and, given the state of the Opposition, that is a distinct possibility. He insists — sounding like an old-fashioned conservative — that stability is a public good in itself, and that simply by virtue of a long-term Labor government, Australia will become a better place. The other — putatively conservative — side might beg to differ. Longevity means consolidation: there's no point going out in a blaze of glory only to have the other mob reverse it all, wiping out a generation of your most promising talent in the process. Been there, done that. Hawke/Keating, not Gillard/Rudd, provides the inspiration for his government. The opportunity to implement lasting change, not to mention build substantial careers, is an enticing promise to a party filled with the pent-up energy of years of Opposition. It's certainly a recipe to quell too much internal argumentation. For now.

It also smacks of a kind of complacency and premature self-congratulation, born of an unshakable belief that Labor, by default, is driven by noble intent — a dangerous assumption, given the new reality where lifelong loyalties to major parties are a thing of the past. The question on the minds of anyone who follows politics is: how deep does the desire for reform go? Or is Labor, as some fear, too risk-averse, and all about the vibe (p. 128)?

The Voice has clearly been a passionate cause for Labor. It was a simple proposition to give constitutional recognition to Indigenous Australians and to provide an avenue for communities to be heard on matters that concern them (p. 48). It is uncontroversial in all other areas of public life that effective policy requires the input of the people it most affects.

Albanese argued that it was a generational opportunity to put Australia on the 'right side of history', a phrase related to that other inspirational mantra — the 'moral arc of history bends towards justice' (p. vi). It's a progressive credo in stark contrast to the alternate, tragic view, one that many Indigenous Australians have good reason to hold, that history is a tale told by the winners, and no more than a succession of conquests, wars, and human tragedies piling up in the rear-view mirror. Choose your metaphor. The one you pick might depend on where you live.

Symbolic gestures are an essential part of national self-understanding, and high-sounding principles no doubt make many supporters feel better, but perhaps if Labor were truly serious about far-reaching reform they could also have committed to nation-building investments in areas that desperately need it. But what was on offer was the Voice. It felt churlish to many to refuse it.

Conservatives have always argued, reasonably, that well-meaning schemes of amelioration can have unexpected consequences that often make things worse. The modern right, with its propensity for the Stalin variant of Godwin's Law, pushed that rationale further, citing a danger to the Constitution and democracy itself. Others warned — apparently without a sense of irony — of the dangers of setting up racial hierarchies in Australian society.

Of course, there were many people on the No side who had deeply considered views on the topic, including many who thought it was not radical enough. But much of what has passed for argument was often little more than dog-whistling to some of the nastier and generically aggrieved elements in Australian society, reawakening and legitimising some of the worst impulses and racial stereotypes from the colonial subconscious.

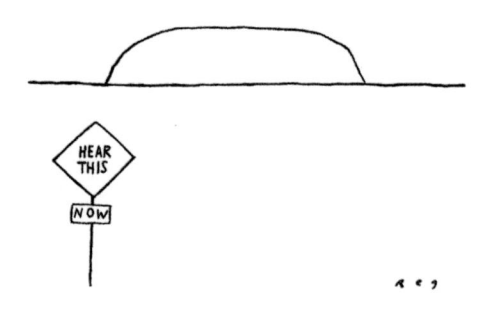

Reg Lynch, *The Sun-Herald*

The amplification of division for short-term political gain has become irresistible. Rejected after a decade in power, the Coalition has no firm ground left to fight on. The Voice became a casualty of this intellectual and ethical bankruptcy, a cynical and opportunist populism of the worst kind. It's a tactic that has no regard for consequences, yet has the advantage of deniability — other people do the dirty work for you. Le Lievre's response (p. 63) has farmer Dutton sowing the seeds for a future harvest of grievance. Unfortunately, liberal impulses — with honourable exceptions — remain timorous and stifled. The question *Have you no decency?* has yet to be asked within the Coalition.

History might not have a right or wrong side — but it does have demographic and social trends. Dutton's right have thrown in with true reactionaries against these shifts. Their usefully vague, all-purpose target, the world of woke, can be wheeled out at every opportunity, whether in the crusade for the defence of gendered pronouns or to excuse war crimes by Aussie heroes (p. 68). All this is so much more fun than serious and thoughtful analysis. While it is unlikely to arrest their extraordinary fall from electoral grace into history's dustbin (p. 11), or provide an answer to their alienation from a changing world so manifestly exposed by the last election, the damage it can do to a historical self-understanding is already plain to see.

Albanese's inherent caution underlies his promise to re-establish trust with voters on key issues, such as the economy and national security, and in government in general. Following the revelations of the Robodebt inquiry, it's easy to understand why this is central to the Labor project. The finding that the tactics of the Income Compliance Program were 'neither fair nor legal' and filled with examples of 'venality, incompetence and cowardice' was an excoriating indictment of the Coalition's legacy, singling out Scott Morrison for special attention (p. 24).

The establishment of the National Anti-Corruption Commission was the fulfilment of a critical election promise (p. 40), delivered with the support of the Teals. The legacy of the Coalition's relaxed ethics filled the lists of referrals submitted to the NACC as soon as the doors opened. No doubt wishing to short-circuit the delegitimisation of such commissions implied by the chorus of support for Gladys Berejiklian, despite the clear findings against her by the NSW ICAC (p. 41), Commissioner Paul Brereton insisted that uncovering corrupt conduct was vital to improving integrity in governance, whether it reached the level of criminality or not. The consequence of outsourcing large swathes of governance to multinational consulting firms and the concomitant deskilling of the public service hit the fan this year with continuing revelations about the conflicts of interest in the large consultancies. The NACC is going to be busy (p. 44).

Brittany Higgins' ordeal continues to illuminate the dark shadows in contemporary gender relations, eating careers and reputations in the process (p. 32). The twists and turns, the charges and the denials, have leant a complexity to the case that has distracted from the fact that everything flowed from an inadequate response to a young woman's allegation of rape.

The Coalition, deeply embarrassed while in government, believed that Labor had amplified and weaponised the case. Sensing the possibility for revenge, they subjected Katie Gallagher to a sustained but ultimately fruitless interrogation. In the ensuing debates, Lidia Thorpe reported that she had been sexually harassed by David Van. Following a well-worn script, his defenders attempted to discredit Thorpe by implying that she was unstable and lacked credibility — a line that seriously backfired when a more 'reliable' woman, former Coalition MP Amanda Stoker, revealed her own experience of him. The response to Thorpe and Higgins' treatment in sections of the media, including the publishing of private texts, serves as a warning of the costs and the retribution in store for reporting rape, let alone 'minor' harassment. The 'clean up' after the Jenkins review into a toxic parliamentary culture is clearly still a work in progress.

The familiar tactic of new administrations — and certainly those with large majorities — is to get the unpopular reform done early on, while the Opposition is on its knees and your credibility remains intact. However, that's not an option if dependability is a central pillar of your identity. The totemic issue for Labor has been its promise to implement the Stage 3 tax cuts accepted in Opposition while trying to close down any chink of light between them and the Morrison government (p. 120). Depending on your perspective, it's commendable trustworthiness or gutless timidity, but the cuts stalk every conversation on social expenditure. They invite a stark interrogation of Labor's priorities and values: tax cuts for the wealthy, or a living wage for jobseekers; more 'no one held back' than 'no one left behind'. Is the once-proud party of egalitarianism now just a bunch of marginally nicer folk than the other lot, running a more efficient version of the same loaded system?

The vertiginous rise in the cost of living and falling wages, with its injurious effects on the most precarious lives — people for whom tax cuts and $3 million super balances have no meaning — have been centre stage this year (p. 98). The anticipation of the monthly inflation figures and the succession of interest-rate rises gave Philip Lowe a notoriety previously enjoyed by state medical officers announcing Covid figures (p. 106).

Was the fundamental problem really about wage spirals? What about the windfall profits reported by large corporations (p. 112)? Pick your villain, but clearly the crude weapons at the Reserve Bank of Australia's disposal have little effect on the deeper causes — the cascading effects of the war in Ukraine, global energy prices, and the post-Covid economy. Beating the least well off over the head with injunctions to toughen up and tighten their belts did not go down well. When the report into the RBA highlighted the dangers of 'groupthink', clearly Lowe's days were numbered (p. 115).

The history of treating housing as a real estate asset rather than a right has set up intractable economic and electoral dilemmas. Albanese — whose public-housing origin story plays such a big part in the confection of his political persona — isn't, according to the Greens, all that strong on reform, after all. They charge that Labor's something-is-better-than-nothing Housing Australia Future Fund is unlikely to touch the sides of an unfolding crisis (p. 102).

While Albanese might regard Max Chandler-Mather as a 'joke', it is dangerous to dismiss the Greens as student politicians demanding unrealistic changes (p. 104). Holding the balance of power in the Senate means that the Greens can hold their ground, resisting threats of a double dissolution. The breakdown of party loyalties and demographic shifts underway won't only hurt the Liberals. Impossible rents are a fundamental concern that will affect the generations to whom Chandler-Mather speaks for years to come. *Why vote Labor if they're indistinguishable from the Coalition* is an electoral pitch potentially damaging to Labor's prospects for long-term majority government.

•

The domestic climate wars might not be completely over, but the Tony Abbott–inspired politicking is (p. 72). After heated negotiations, the government delivered its promised climate change bill with an emissions-reduction target of 43 per cent by the end of the decade, net zero by 2050, and stricter approvals for new fossil fuel projects (p. 74). Despite the Greens holding the balance of power in the Senate, their ambit claim of a 75 per cent reduction by 2030 and a ban on new fossil fuel projects failed.

However, the pressure for more serious action on what they regard as Labor's limited ambitions will continue. Expect to hear more criticism of naive utopians and perfect-is-the-enemy-of-the-good charges against the Greens, the tired recycled cliché dating from their rejection of Kevin Rudd's climate policy (p. 88).

Meanwhile, from the Indus Valley to Maui, crazy climatic extremes continue to drown and burn the world. As the CEO of Chamber of Minerals and Energy said, reacting to an inconvenient climate protest, everyone has a right to feel safe in their own home (p. 78). Many don't. Concerted international action is hamstrung by conflict, formidable vested interests, and a deep structural dependence on fossil fuels. Despite the mandatory optimism, the annual COP travelling circus has become almost irrelevant to the hardcore geopolitical reality of energy economics (p. 82).

Matt Golding, *The Age*

•

Everyone seems to have an opinion on the arcane operations of the RBA, but involving people in an apparently less immediate argument about our place in the world is much harder. Yet the momentous and transformational foreign-policy decisions made this year could make all such domestic conversations appear provincial.

Richard Marles, the man charged by the previous government with everything from appeasement to being a Beijing sleeper agent, has settled into a comfortable role, talking up undying mateship in Washington and locking in hugely consequential weapons contracts that tie us for generations to the interests and vagaries of a fractious US.

The AUKUS commitment was made in the absence of a serious national conversation to define our vital national interests, our future security, or the role of regional states — most of whom incline to diplomacy rather than hardware. It is taken for granted that Australian and US interests, now and into the future, will coalesce (p. 138).

And while we have learned, at great expense, that the current Chinese leadership inclines to punishment rather than cultivation in its foreign policy, the precise nature of the threat to Australia has never — beyond scary newspaper graphics — been properly articulated (p. 150). What is clear, though, is that we are well beyond ANZUS. The agreement to host offensive US nuclear submarines and B52 bombers makes Australian cities a nuclear target in any escalating American war with China. Whether we're engaging in deterrence or provocation, the consequences are never discussed. The cost to our sovereignty, despite claims to the contrary, seems indisputable. The phrase 'sleepwalking into war' is apposite.

While the cabinet was happy to rubber-stamp a plan hatched in the fevered brains of a clapped-out government intent on a national security wedge, a typically hyperbolic attack by Paul Keating attempted to kick a hole in this shallowly arrived at consensus (p. 148). He was, of course, charged with being out of touch and stuck in the 1990s.

But, in a brilliant riff on Labor's slogan, Dyson references a compulsive repetition of that other deep-seated historical psychodrama — the fear of being left behind, abandoned in a scary Asian world by our once-powerful Anglophone friends (back cover).

Did someone say international rules-based order? This year marked the 70th anniversary of the Korean armistice; the 50th anniversary of Australia's departure from the Vietnam War; the 20th anniversary of the invasion of Iraq; and two years since the departure of Western forces from Afghanistan. No doubt, many of the heirs of the legacies of those wars would agree with Henry Kissinger, on his 100th birthday, that it can be more dangerous being America's friend than its enemy (p. 130).

A misplaced nostalgia for the moral simplicity of the Cold War is there in the autocracy/democracy binary trotted out to frame the current geopolitical volatility. But as states compete for the diminishing resources of an overcrowded planet, this new world order is increasingly determined by specific national interests rather than by acquiescence to a single great power. Hence the difficulty in building a consensus beyond the West on Russia and its continuing atrocities in Ukraine (p. 162).

China and Russia, of course are autocratic, deeply undemocratic states (p. 160). But the Western tick of approval, always highly selectively applied, is increasingly meaningless as the very question of democracy is brought into question. The US can hardly claim to be a shining city on a hill in a world mired in darkness when one of its major parties remains in thrall to a former president who conspired to overturn a legitimate election (p. 178). We're prepared to forgive Narendra Modi, the leader of world's largest democracy and Albo's new best friend, for his profoundly divisive sectarian vision of Indian society (p. 168). Discussion of Israel's democratic failings, despite its creeping annexation of the West Bank and extreme ethno-nationalist shift, remain hamstrung by a sensitivity not granted to other states (p. 170).

Claims of undying friendship and shared values notwithstanding, we will still be here with our geographical reality long after the US decides its vital interests lie elsewhere and the costs of regional hegemony are too high, and rides its metaphorical choppers out of the mess it's left behind for the military and economic palisades of fortress America. Just maybe, strategies to avoid cataclysmic future wars should be prioritised over the dangerous chimera of an imagined US 'rules-based order'.

•

Many of us approach the future with an underlying sense of dread — if global conflict doesn't get us, global heating will (p. 7). Indeed, the world we have made increasingly presents us with choices constrained between lesser evils. Labor presents its policy options as the difficult but necessary decisions of a 'mature nation'. Responsible, non-ideological, grown-up. Many see in this pragmatism an unimaginative but more efficient and presentable business-as-usual managerialism — the dying embers of Labor's forgotten soul. But looking good compared to the previous lot won't sustain them for long.

Two different but emblematic experiences illustrate our failure to adequately address our past, and thus understand our present: as a young Indigenous boy, you are more likely to go to jail than university; as a whistleblower, you are more likely to be put on trial for revealing war crimes than committing them, as David McBride's continuing ordeal shows (p. 134).

Right sides of history and moral arcs are fictions, albeit useful ones — guides to action rather than indicators of destiny. The past can't be changed, but symbolic gestures — looking back with honesty and humility at that pile of failure and suffering in the rear-view mirror — is a necessary but only preliminary step to bending that moral arc a few more degrees, and ensuring the future isn't just more of the same.

— Russ Radcliffe

Fiona Katauskas, *The Guardian*

Matt Golding, *The Age*

Andrew Weldon, *The Big Issue*

'While the world was getting more uncertain, we had been growing more vulnerable. Domestic policies — and policy vacuums — accelerated rather than alleviated this problem ... Our mission is to redefine and reform our economy and institutions in ways that make our people and communities more resilient, and our society and democracy stronger as well.'
— Jim Chalmers

'After a decade of inaction, you can't simply wish things to happen.'
— Anthony Albanese

'The wasted decade behind us and the challenges immediately ahead are all part of a long chain of rupture ... disparate shocks interacting so that the whole is even more overwhelming than the sum of its parts .... We can see this in how the three crises have played out. The global financial crisis, never fully resolved, defining our fragility as the pandemic crisis hit. Then a third with its roots in the inadequate response to the previous two.'
— Jim Chalmers

The Interview.

"Well, Prime Minister, what's it gonna be? Culture Wars and the Politics of Envy, or Backflips and Broken Promises?"

Cathy Wilcox, *The Sydney Morning Herald*

'I believe that Labor should be the natural party of government — that our values sit with a majority of Australians, the values of a fair go and not leaving people behind, but also of not holding people back. Those are values of aspiration for a better life.'
— Anthony Albanese

'My theory of governing is people will cop big things done slowly and little things done quickly, but not big things done quickly or little things done slowly.'
— Jim Chalmers

'What isn't the right thing to do is to put forward positions that can't be delivered … That leads to disillusionment and undermines the integrity of what you're putting forward.'
— Anthony Albanese

Jon Kudelka, *The Saturday Paper*

Jon Kudelka, *The Saturday Paper*

the dustbin of history

THE MARTYRDOM OF SAINT SCOTT OF THE BACK BENCH

Jon Kudelka, *The Saturday Paper*

'Going back to being a quiet Australian in the Shire — that's what I'm looking forward to.'
 — Scott Morrison

'Mr Morrison now has to get back to first principles — he is there to represent the people of Cook. If his heart's not in that, it's probably time for him to move on and let someone who does have the passion and the fire in the belly.'
 — David Littleproud

'As Prime Minister my awareness of issues regarding national security and the national interest was broader than that known to individual Ministers and certainly to the Inquiry. This limits the ability for third parties to draw definitive conclusions on such matters.'
 — Scott Morrison

Dean Alston,
The West Australian

John Shakespeare,
The Sydney Morning Herald

Megan Herbert, *The Age*

Peter Broelman, *www.broelman.com.au*

Jon Kudelka, *The Saturday Paper*

'The silent majority, the forgotten people … are fed up with bodies like the Civil Liberties Council and the Refugee Action Collective and certainly the dictatorship of the trade union movement.'
— Peter Dutton, maiden parliamentary speech

'The time to bloodlet after our defeat a year ago is over. The time to sook and moan is done.'
— Sussan Ley

'I think the party needs to stop ideological dog-whistling and return to centrist Liberal values … We've seen an infiltration … of right-wing religious conservatism that's … turned it into something it was never conceived to be.'
— Bridget Archer

'I've chosen to play tackle, not touch, when I came into this business.'
— Peter Dutton

'[Peter Dutton has] exactly what it takes to be an effective opposition leader: courage, convictions, and temperament.'
— Tony Abbott

THE NEW IMAGE...

OLD ... HAPPY   ... ANGRY   ... SAD

NEW ... EMPATHETIC   .. APOLOGETIC ..   .. APOPLECTIC

Alan Moir, *www.moir.com.au*

LAPPING AT THE DOOR...

COALITION

IRRELEVANCE

John Farmer, *The Mercury*

David Rowe, *Australian Financial Review*

'Too much of the government's effort is concentrated on capital cities. We are the party of regional and rural Australia ... We've got to make sure that our policies provide support to people living in regional Australia.'
— Peter Dutton

'The Liberal Party, founded in 1944, is the most successful political party in Australia's history, but if we pursue a strategy of ignoring city seats and focus only on the suburbs and the regions ... we will become the doughnut party, a party ... incapable of pitching our tent across the country as we have done so successfully in the past 75 years.'
— Andrew Bragg

'We've got to have a revolution, really, to take the party back ... I don't think Menzies would be particularly disappointed with my efforts.'
— Bridget Archer

First Dog on the Moon, *The Guardian*

Alan Moir, *www.moir.com.au*

Reg Lynch, *The Sun-Herald*

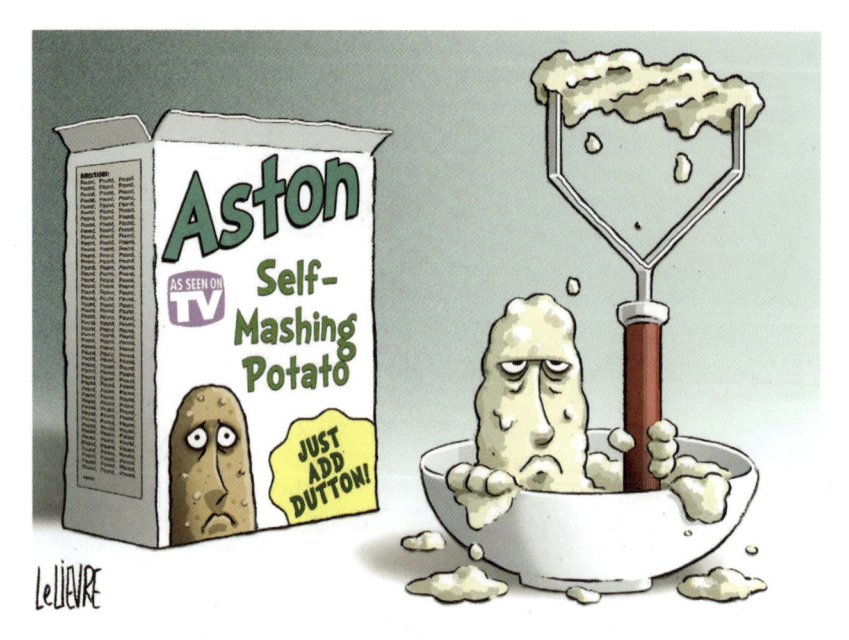

Glen Le Lievre, *Australian Financial Review*

Peter Broelman, *The Echidna*

David Rowe, *Australian Financial Review*

'Peter Dutton has the rare distinction of being a populist without actually being popular.'
— Angus Grigg, 2018

'The Victorian Liberal Party is like the space shuttle *Columbia* slamming into the *Hindenburg* and then landing on the deck of the *Titanic*.'
— Tony Barry

'By not winning the election, we've failed that test that has been set for us by the Victorian people … That's the reality. Now, the question is how we rebuild from here, the policies that we have, the brand rebuilding that we need to do in Victoria, and it is a very significant issue for us.'
— Peter Dutton

human intelligence 101

Andrew Dyson, *The Age*

'Should we let machines flood our information channels with propaganda and untruth? Should we automate away all the jobs, including the fulfilling ones? Should we develop nonhuman minds that might eventually outnumber, outsmart, obsolete, and replace us? Should we risk loss of control of our civilization? Such decisions must not be delegated to unelected tech leaders.'
   — open letter, Future of Life Institute

'Mitigating the risk of extinction from AI should be a global priority alongside other societal-scale risks such as pandemics and nuclear war.'
   — statement by key AI leaders

Matt Golding, *The Age*

John Farmer, *The Mercury*

Mark Knight, *Herald Sun*

'The Australian Signals Directorate's (ASD) Australian Cyber Security Centre (ACSC) has seen broad targeting of Australians and Australian organisations, through rapid exploitation of technical vulnerabilities by state actors and cybercriminals seeking to exploit weaknesses and steal sensitive data.'
— Clare O'Neil

'Cybercrime is the break and enter of the 21st century, and personal information is being used as currency.'
— Reece Kershaw, AFP

'All we have to go on at present is the word of a criminal who had no hesitation to dump more than 10,000 records publicly. Plus, the vulnerability as it's been described is so trivial it's entirely possible it was exploited by other parties as well.'
— Troy Hunt

'The smartest and toughest people in our country are going to hack the hackers.'
— Clare O'Neil

Megan Herbert, *The Age*

Mark David, *independentaustralia.net*

David Pope, *The Canberra Times*

'Robodebt was a crude and cruel mechanism, neither fair nor legal, and it made many people feel like criminals. In essence, people were traumatised on the off-chance they might owe money. It was a costly failure of public administration, in both human and economic terms.'
— Commissioner Catherine Holmes

'We will find you, we will track you down, and you will have to repay those debts, and you may end up in prison.'
— Alan Tudge

'The media strategy we developed was to run a counter-narrative in the more friendly media such as *The Australian* and the tabloids, which we knew were interested in running stories about … supposed dole-bludgers.'
— Rachelle Miller

'Are all those people with their hands in the taxpayer pocket in genuine need? … Keep at it, you're doing a great job.'
— Chris Smith

Mark Knight, *Herald Sun*

Matt Bissett-Johnson, *Melbourne Observer*

Cathy Wilcox, *The Sydney Morning Herald*

'It is remarkable how little interest there seems to have been in ensuring the scheme's legality, how rushed its implementation was, how little thought was given to how it would affect welfare recipients and the lengths to which public servants were prepared to go to oblige ministers on a quest for savings.'
— Commissioner Catherine Holmes

'I didn't know the full context in relation to the legalities ... It just had not crossed my mind until I read about it in the newspaper.'
— Alan Tudge

Stuart Robert: 'I had a massive personal misgiving, yes, but I'm still a cabinet minister.'
Commissioner Holmes: 'Yes, but it doesn't compel you to say things that you don't believe to be true, surely?'

'[The royal commission] exposed a soullessness and hollowness in parts of the public service and ministries.'
— Bill Shorten

Matt Golding, *The Age*

Mark Knight, *Herald Sun*

David Rowe, *Australian Financial Review*

'Any self-respecting politician having the sort of detailed, forensic examination and assessment made by this royal commission would be embarrassed, humiliated.'
— Bill Shorten

'The Commission rejects as untrue Mr Morrison's evidence that he was told that income averaging as contemplated in the Executive Minute was an established practice and a "foundational way" in which DHS worked.'
— Royal Commission

'The findings which are adverse to me are based upon a fundamental misunderstanding of how government operates.'
— Scott Morrison

'The Member for Cook is a bottomless well of self-pity and not a drop of mercy for all of the real victims of Robodebt.'
— Bill Shorten

David Pope, *The Canberra Times*

"I DON'T ACCEPT THE PREMISE OF YOUR QUESTION."

Glen Le Lievre, *Patreon*

David Pope, *The Canberra Times*

'I am confident that the Commission has served the purpose of bringing into the open an extraordinary saga, illustrating a myriad of ways that things can go wrong through venality, incompetence, and cowardice.'
— Commissioner Catherine Holmes

'I caution the glee of the prime minister and Bill Shorten … They've sought to politicise this issue from day one.'
— Peter Dutton

'There could have been a hint of empathy from Peter Dutton, but there was none … a refusal to even say that anything wrong happened here in spite of the very clear evidence.'
— Anthony Albanese

'I say to the government, instead of trying to distract attention from their own failings by relentlessly pursuing these transparently partisan campaigns against me, they get on with the job they promised to do and are failing to do.'
— Scott Morrison

Glen Le Lievre, *Patreon*

Brett Lethbridge, *The Courier Mail*

we'll need a bigger truck

Andrew Dyson, *The Age*

'This is what happens when you weaponise a rape allegation … This matter always should have been left to the criminal justice system … there appears to have been collusion with senior members of the Labor Party with the media.'
 — Michaelia Cash

'As you know, the Gaetjens review was commissioned by Mr Morrison, and the findings of that review never released. I think that it is appropriate that the former government answer questions about the way that review was conducted and why its findings were never released.'
 — Jenny McAllister

Reg Lynch, *The Sun-Herald*

Reg Lynch, *The Sun-Herald*

David Rowe, *Australian Financial Review*

'It's increasingly clear that a group of Labor operatives conspired to maximise the damage. It was absolutely brazen. Labor used an alleged rape victim for political purposes.'
— Peter Dutton

'I have at all times been guided by the bravery and courage of a young woman who chose to speak up and about an alleged incident in her workplace. I have always acted ethically and with basic human decency on all matters related to Ms Higgins. I will continue to do so.'
— Katy Gallagher

'We've had enough shit shoved down our throats. It's a classic beware the man to lose … I've got nothing to lose.'
— Bruce Lehrmann

Brett Lethbridge, *The Courier Mail*

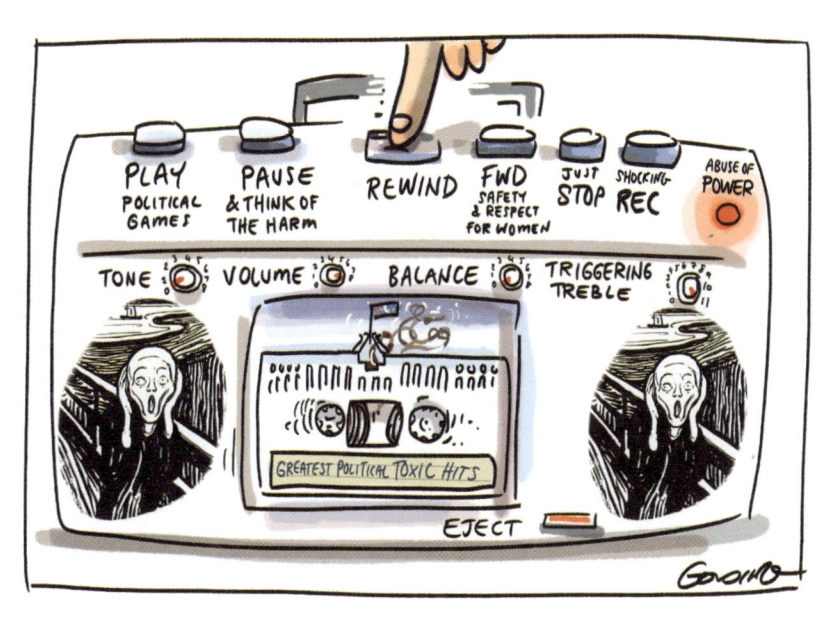

Matt Golding, *The Age*

Jon Kudelka, *The Saturday Paper*

Sean Leahy, *The Courier Mail*

Cathy Wilcox, *The Sydney Morning Herald*

'The central point here is that a young woman made an allegation that she had been sexually assaulted in her workplace and that it had been inappropriately investigated, even covered up by her employers.'
— Tanya Plibersek

'Utterly shattered … that my good reputation can be so wantonly savaged without due process or accountability.'
— David Van

'I think Senator Thorpe has lots of issues, and some of those and her own conduct have been well documented.'
— Peter Dutton

'I would have preferred that the matter be resolved privately and finally — as I thought it was. However, following Senator Thorpe's allegations, it is now clear that is no longer tenable.'
— Amanda Stoker

David Pope, *The Canberra Times*

David Pope, *The Canberra Times*

> YOU HAVE THE RIGHT **NOT** TO REMAIN SILENT BUT ANYTHING YOU SAY CAN AND WILL BE USED AGAINST YOU IN A COURT OF PUBLIC OPINION...
>
> SEXUAL ASSAULT REPORTING UNIT

Fiona Katauskas, *The Guardian*

'It's been horrible. I became the perpetrator. I became the person that was demonised … I had a media pile on that day. And it wasn't until a white woman stood up and said, *Yeah, this happened to me, too* that the media took notice.'
— Lidia Thorpe

'It's something that women are vigilant about all the time. You know, they're conscious of where they are, what their surroundings are, who's there.'
— Bridget Archer

'I'm absolutely disgusted with the game-playing going on in the Parliament right now.'
— Sarah Hanson-Young

'And you wonder why women don't speak out. You wonder why we are silenced.'
— Lidia Thorpe

Glen Le Lievre, *Australian Financial Review*

'[Berejiklian] engaged in serious corrupt conduct by breaching public trust in 2016 and 2017 ... [She was] in a position of a conflict of interest between her public duty and her private interest.'
— ICAC

'She chose a bum, basically, and he was a bad guy ... Her integrity is not in question. She's not a corrupt person.'
— Peter Dutton

'So it has taken ICAC two years to tell us that Gladys Berejiklian has not broken the law.'
— Matt Kean

'It is precisely in the area where it may not be possible to establish criminal conduct ... that the commission's [NACC] work can be most important in enhancing integrity by investigating and exposing corrupt conduct.'
— Paul Brereton

David Pope, *The Canberra Times*

Matt Bissett-Johnson, *Melbourne Observer*

Matt Golding, *The Age*

'The people of the Commonwealth [of Australia] are no longer prepared to tolerate practices which might once have been the subject of, if not acceptance, at least acquiescence.'
— Paul Brereton

'If we want the trust of the Australian people, if we want them to trust in government and democracy, we have to show bad behaviour won't be swept under the rug.'
— Helen Haines

'We need to see the relationships, the behaviours, the individuals involved really brought to account, and it needs the resources and the independence of an organisation like the NACC.'
— Barbara Pocock

'Laws are pointless if they are not enforced … And a law which is not enforced soon becomes a dead letter.'
— Paul Brereton

John Farmer, *The Mercury*

Fiona Katauskas, *The Echidna*

Andrew Dyson, *The Age*

'We were aggressive in telling these relationships they needed to act early, heavily helped by accuracy of the intelligence that Peter Collins was able to supply us and our analysis of the politics.'
— PwC partner, anon

'This is a disgraceful breach of trust, a sickening example of a lack of integrity … [that] stretches across the globe.'
— Deborah O'Neill

'If a case such as this can't be investigated by the NACC, then we clearly have a problem with our brand new anti-corruption watchdog.'
— Barbara Pocock

'Dracula at the blood bank, you think, Minister?'
— David Shoebridge

David Pope, *The Canberra Times*

Jon Kudelka, *The Saturday Paper*

David Pope, *The Canberra Times*

'They were voracious, greedy, lying scoundrels, and they thought they could get away with it — and they probably would have, without alert journalists and an alert Senate.'
— Barbara Pocock

'This is a company that, let's be clear, has stolen confidential Treasury information and monetised that to help their clients actually avoid paying tax in Australia.'
— Nick McKim

'PwC have been circling like vultures to get these contracts, haven't they?'
— David Shoebridge

'It's no longer just about PwC … this is the global business model the industry is engaged in. They don't come in just to provide internal advice; they come in to provide advice on government policy. They tell you to privatise or to put in place commercial models, and then you need them to enact those changes.'
— James Guthrie

First Dog on the Moon, *The Guardian*

the right side of history

Peter Broelman, *The Echidna*

'We cannot aim low. We must not dampen our aspirations for change. We must work hard, as Lingiari did … We must have courage, as Lingiari did.'
— Thomas Mayo

'We're here to draw a line in the sand and say this has to change.'
— Marcia Langton

'It's about being on the right side of history. And Peter Dutton has in recent days reflected on what it is like to be on the wrong side of history, after walking out on the apology to the Stolen Generations.'
— Linda Burney

Alan Moir, *www.moir.com.au*

Reg Lynch, *The Sun-Herald*

David Pope, *The Canberra Times*

'The Yes vote is to allow for a powerless voice to go into the Constitution … So I can't support something that gives us no power, and I certainly cannot support a No campaign that is looking more like a white-supremacy campaign that is causing a lot of harm … So I'm considering to abstain from the up-and-coming vote.'
— Lidia Thorpe

'There is a welcome-to-country message every morning; it used to be the prayers first, and they've reversed that. When I'm in the Parliament and that happens, I turn my back.'
— Pauline Hanson

'Asking Australians to avoid highlighting race in the voice debate is like asking someone to avoid getting wet walking through monsoonal rains. This is not the fault of everyday Australians but of the unyielding activist class that for the past decade has doused petrol on the flames of identity politics.'
— Jacinta Nampijinpa Price

Mark Knight, *Herald Sun*

Johannes Leak, *The Australian*

Peter Broelman, *The Echidna*

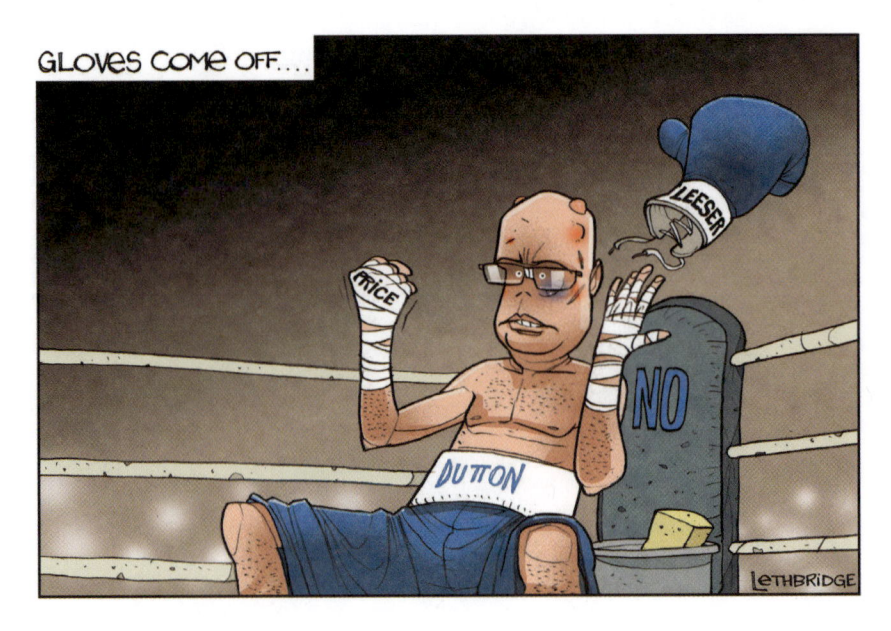

Brett Lethbridge, *The Courier Mail*

Matt Bissett-Johnson, *Melbourne Observer*

'My resignation today as a frontbencher is … about trying to keep faith with the very chords of belief and belonging that are part of who I am. Keeping faith with the first peoples of this land who want to have a stake in their own futures with structural change in our Constitution to help improve the quality of their lives.'
— Julian Leeser

'I still believe in the Liberal Party values, but I don't believe in what the Liberals have become. Aboriginal people are reaching out to be heard but the Liberals have rejected their invitation.'
— Ken Wyatt

'Ken wouldn't have taken this decision lightly. He would have angst over it. And I'm sure he would be very disappointed that his party has shown absolutely no regard for the Aboriginal people, their leadership, and their efforts to find an accommodation with the Australian people through a Voice to Parliament being embedded in the Constitution.'
— Patrick Dodson

David Rowe, *Australian Financial Review*

'At a time when we need to unite the country, this prime minister's proposal will permanently divide us by race … Changing our constitution to enshrine a Voice will take our country backwards, not forwards … It will have an Orwellian effect where all Australians are equal, but some Australians are more equal than others.'
— Peter Dutton

'I couldn't sleep last night. I was haunted by dreams, and the spectre of the Peter Dutton Liberal Party's Judas betrayal of our country … I see Peter Dutton as an undertaker, preparing the grave to bury Uluru.'
— Noel Pearson

'I take time out because we have shown again that our history — our hard truth — is too big, too fragile, too precious for the media. The media sees only battle lines, not bridges. It sees only politics.'
— Stan Grant

Mark David, *independentaustralia.net*

Alan Moir, *www.moir.com.au*

David Pope, *The Canberra Times*

'I don't think this is in our country's best interest. I have spent literally months ... trying to understand what it is the prime minister is proposing. We cannot get the basic detail out of them. We think it is deliberate.'
— Peter Dutton

'If you are a leader or advocate for the Yes case, you have a responsibility to listen to the legitimate questions of those who doubt. And if you are a leader or advocate for the No case, then you have a responsibility to listen to the aspirations of Indigenous Australians who see value in a Voice. No matter where we are in this debate, we all must find a way to walk a mile in another's shoes.'
— Julian Leeser

'A powerless voice. We have fought over 200 years against colonisation. The Constitution is an illegal document. It's illegal. The occupation in this country is illegal. You're following the King. And now, poor little black fellas are begging for a seat at the table and all we get is to become advisers with no power. Well, I'm ashamed. I'm ashamed. That we're not standing here for a treaty or for some truth to happen in this country.'
— Lidia Thorpe

John Farmer,
The Mercury

Matt Golding,
The Age

David Pope, *The Canberra Times*

'This is about whether we as a country can be optimistic, can be enlarged, can come to terms with the fullness and richness of our history, can express our pride in sharing this continent with the oldest continuous culture on earth, or whether we shrink in on ourselves.'
— Anthony Albanese

'We can't give a special voice to the First Australians without establishing a hierarchy of descent; or indeed, a pecking order among all the victims of history.'
— Tony Abbott

'If you've seen any blackfellas on the streets there, would you say they are more equal than other Australians?'
— Noel Pearson

'If we put the Voice into the Constitution, to my mind, we're effectively announcing an apartheid-type state, where some citizens have more legal rights or more rights in general than others.'
— Cory Bernardi

Cathy Wilcox, *The Sydney Morning Herald*

Fiona Katauskas, *The Echidna*

David Rowe, *Australian Financial Review*

'We implore all editors and journalists to recognise this for what it actually is: a deliberate decision by key members of the No campaign to flout facts in this campaign.'
— Uluru Dialogues

'We have just heard in one speech, every bit of disinformation and misinformation and scare campaigns that exist in this debate.'
— Linda Burney

'This disregard for truth, fact, and the most basic of journalistic standards must be of concern in any democracy, yet it goes unchecked as the Murdoch empire extends its reach.'
— Malcolm Turnbull and Sharan Burrow

David Pope, *The Canberra Times*

Cathy Wilcox, *The Sydney Morning Herald*

Peter Broelman, *www.broelman.com.au*

Brett Lethbridge, *The Courier Mail*

Glen Le Lievre, *Patreon*

'IS STAN GRANT DOING "BLACK FACE"? If so, why?'
— David Adler

'It was shocking, when I first saw these things, the intensity of it, just the sheer volume of hatred. But, at a certain point, it just started to put more fire in my belly.'
— Thomas Mayo

'The racist trope of Thomas Mayo in today's full-page *AFR* ad has no place in Australian politics. It's a throwback to the Jim Crow era of the deep south.'
— Matt Kean

'The Liberals are a small racist rump sliding into irrelevance.'
— Adam Bandt

Cathy Wilcox, *The Sydney Morning Herald*

'The Voice will be a decisive step towards moving Australia from the old settler/native society to one, perhaps, where we are all natives of Australia.'
— Noel Pearson

'If you're a young Indigenous bloke today, you're more likely to go to jail than university.'
— Jason Clare

'I believe we need a 2023 Intervention.'
— David Littleproud

'They don't want the best for Indigenous Australians. They want the rent paid. They want to pay their respects to the elders of the Communist Party. They want to abolish Australia Day. They want reparations.'
— Jacinta Nampijinpa Price

David Pope, *The Canberra Times*

Mark Knight, *Herald Sun*

Peter Broelman, *The Echidna*

Reg Lynch, *The Sun-Herald*

Cathy Wilcox, *The Sydney Morning Herald*

'I do hold the view that the luckiest thing that happened to this country was being colonised by the British.'
— John Howard

'If this was an invasion, it was a bloody good one. Because we have built a wonderful liberal society, which would never have been built but for a civilisation arriving here, overtaking people who were our forebears. We all were hunter-gatherers, but we moved on.'
— Gary Johns

'I would encourage No voters to maintain the rage.'
— John Howard

'We need to find common ground as Australians … No great nation has ever been built by dividing it.'
— Julian Leeser

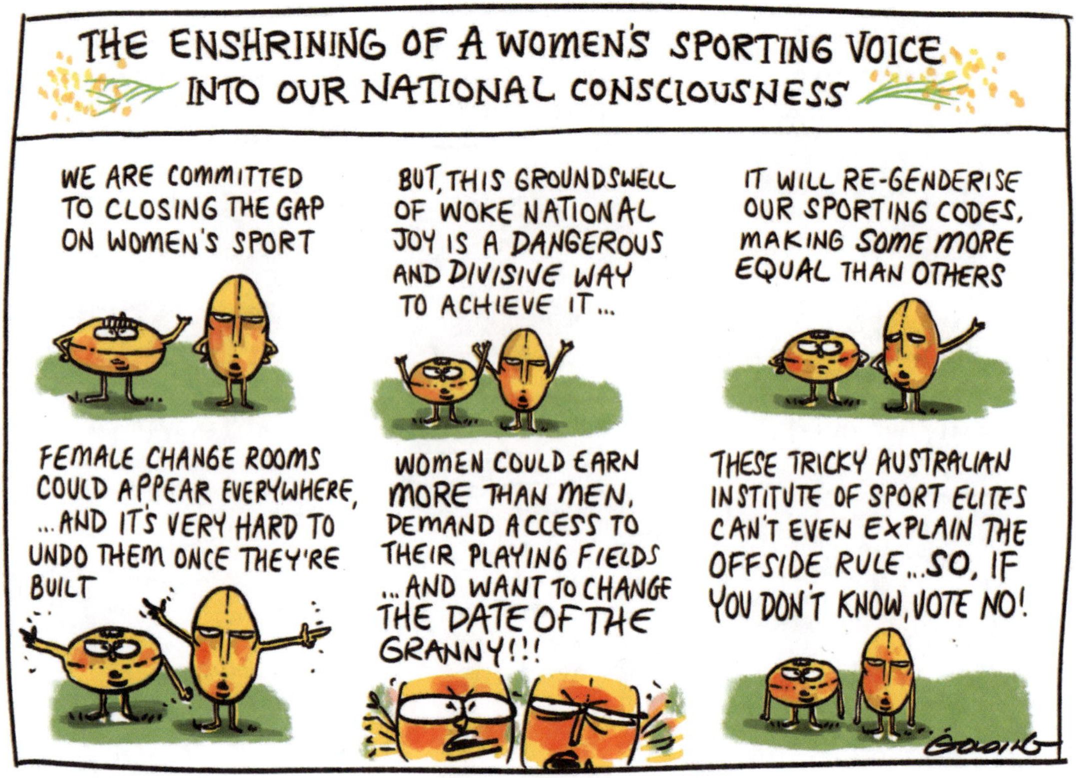

THE ENSHRINING OF A WOMEN'S SPORTING VOICE INTO OUR NATIONAL CONSCIOUSNESS

WE ARE COMMITTED TO CLOSING THE GAP ON WOMEN'S SPORT

BUT, THIS GROUNDSWELL OF WOKE NATIONAL JOY IS A DANGEROUS AND *DIVISIVE* WAY TO ACHIEVE IT...

IT WILL RE-GENDERISE OUR SPORTING CODES, MAKING *SOME MORE EQUAL THAN OTHERS*

FEMALE CHANGE ROOMS COULD APPEAR EVERYWHERE, ...AND IT'S VERY HARD TO UNDO THEM ONCE THEY'RE BUILT

WOMEN COULD EARN MORE THAN MEN, DEMAND ACCESS TO THEIR PLAYING FIELDS ...AND WANT TO CHANGE THE DATE OF THE GRANNY!!!

THESE TRICKY AUSTRALIAN INSTITUTE OF SPORT ELITES CAN'T EVEN EXPLAIN THE OFFSIDE RULE...SO, IF YOU DON'T KNOW, VOTE NO!

Matt Golding, *The Age*

'Go to Australia, which has now become one of the wokest places on earth.'
— Nigel Farage

'I hate to tell you folks, but woke equals fascism — pure and simple.'
— Rowan Dean

'Wokeness is a virus more dangerous than any pandemic hands down.'
— Nikki Haley

'It's time the left pushed back against woke. Afraid of being branded a racist, misogynist, or transphobe, the left has been browbeaten into silence by woke activists, even though the left enabled the modern movements for black rights, gay rights, and feminism.'
— Clive Hamilton

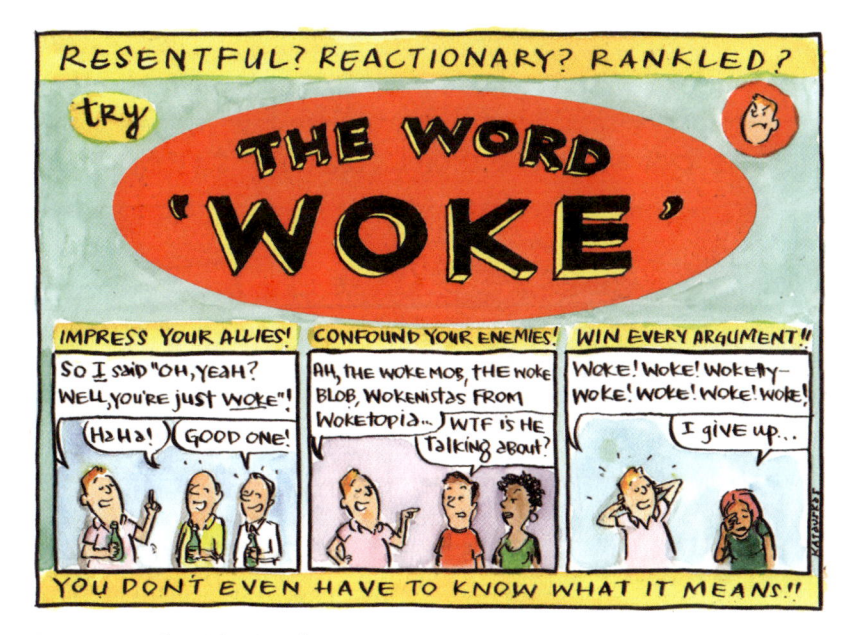

Fiona Katauskas, *The Guardian*

Johannes Leak, *The Australian*

Fiona Katauskas, *The Guardian*

'Visas of Medevac Refugees were renewed today. Only for 6 months. They want us to leave Australia. No rights to study or get a qualification yet. Same shit, different party. Happy New Year.'
— @AzimiMoz

'I'm aware some key contract subcontractors … were the ones making the corrupt payments. We were strongly pressured to take on some of those subcontractors … It was said to me by Home Affairs officials … that if we were just to take them on as a subcontractor, then we would have no troubles.'
— former director, Paladin

'We suspected that there were funny deals involving politicians behind the scenes. Now that it is clear the extent of those dealings, I'm outraged.'
— Nauru official, anon

Fiona Katauskas, *The Guardian*

Cathy Wilcox, *The Sydney Morning Herald*

and bizarrely, the frogs...

Matt Golding, *The Age*

'The era of global warming has ended; the era of global boiling has arrived.'
— António Guterres

'We knew by the mid-1990s that lurking in the tails of our climate-model projections were monsters: monstrous heatwaves, catastrophic extreme rainfall and floods, subcontinental-scale wildfires, rapid icesheet collapse raising sea level metres within a century.'
— Bill Hare

Glen Le Lievre,
Patreon

Fiona Katauskas,
The Guardian

Andrew Weldon, *The Big Issue*

'It is in our interest to reduce greenhouse gas emissions rapidly, substantially, and in a sustained way. It is also in our interest to put in place large and integrated programs for climate adaptation to deal with the climate change impacts we can't avoid. Taking action to reduce emissions and to adapt to climate change will give us hope. Do we really want the alternative?'
— Prof. Mark Howden

'Consumers are now, more than ever, making purchasing decisions on environmental grounds … Unfortunately, it appears that rather than making legitimate changes to their practices and procedures, some businesses are relying on false or misleading claims.'
— Catriona Lowe, ACCC

'This is the first time ASIC has taken an Australian entity to court regarding alleged greenwashing conduct, and it reflects our continuing efforts to ensure sustainability-related claims made by financial institutions are accurate.'
— Sarah Court, ASIC

Megan Herbert, *The Age*

Johannes Leak, *The Australian*

Matt Golding, *The Age*

'The catastrophic floods impacted 33 million people, more than half our women and children ... and ravaged all four corners of Pakistan. We became a victim of something with which we had nothing to do, and of course it was a manmade disaster ... How on earth can one expect from us that we will undertake this gigantic task on our own?'
— Shehbaz Sharif

'What is playing out all over the world right now is entirely consistent with what scientists expect. No one wants to be right about this. But if I'm honest, I am stunned by the ferocity of the impacts we are currently experiencing.'
— Joëlle Gergis

'They can't stop these fires. I mean, they could have 50,000 firefighters there now and it's not going to change it. We could have 200 more air tankers. Are they going to be able to stop these fires that are going? No.'
— Steve Pyne

Cathy Wilcox, *The Sydney Morning Herald*

Andrew Weldon, *The Medical Republic*

Jon Kudelka, *The Saturday Paper*

'Climate protesters are being subjected to vindictive legal action by Australian authorities that is restricting the rights to freedom of peaceful assembly and expression.'
— Sophie McNeill

'Everyone has a right to feel safe in their own home, and any actions that threaten this right must be condemned.'
— Rebecca Tomkinson, Chamber of Minerals and Energy

'All you need to do is sit down on a road to participate; you don't need to wear a fancy costume.'
— Violet CoCo

'They are shooting at the fire alarms rather than putting out the fire.'
— Blockade Australia

'It might be too slow, but the odds are the trajectory is loaded with people who are going to take action through their vote, even if they don't through joining the protests in the street.'
— Bob Brown

Fiona Katauskas, *The Echidna*

Jon Kudelka, *The Saturday Paper*

Judy Horacek, *The Australia Institute*

'Just days ago this wonder of nature, centuries old but still unimaginably strong and youthful, was alive and a natural wonder. Today the tree's death is a national disgrace: it was publicly subsidised and entirely unnecessary.'
— Bob Brown

Judy Horacek,
The Australia Institute

Judy Horacek,
The Australia Institute

Jon Kudelka, *The Saturday Paper*

'The whole idea of annual climate carnivals was probably not the best means of promoting serious action on global heating, but their hijacking by the fossil fuel sector, and failure, year on year, to do the job they were set up to do, surely means that COP is no longer fit for purpose.'
— Bill McGuire

'It's not enough to play to the gallery but act as if they really want to save the planet and not hide behind 2050 net-zero targets, which will bust the remaining carbon budget for 1.5c.'
— Meena Raman

'I welcome the decision to establish a loss and damage fund and to operationalise it in the coming period … Clearly, this will not be enough, but it is a much-needed political signal to rebuild broken trust. The voices of those on the frontlines of the climate crisis must be heard.'
— António Guterres

'This is not about accepting charity … This is a down payment on investment in our futures, and in climate justice.'
— Sherry Rehman

David Pope, *The Canberra Times*

First Dog on the Moon, *The Guardian*

Megan Herbert, *The Age*

David Pope, *The Canberra Times*

'The fact is this: if our reforms are passed, there will be a scheme to ensure emissions come down from big emitters, whether they be old or new … If they don't pass, there will be no such scheme. It will be business as usual.'
— Chris Bowen

'Negotiating with Labor is like negotiating with the political wing of the coal and gas corporations. Labor seems more afraid of the coal and gas corporations than the climate collapse.'
— Adam Bandt

'Are you willing to make the climate change worse by approving projects for your corporate mates?'
— Elizabeth Watson-Brown

'Because of that level of ambition, and the breadth and variety of sectors covered, it's necessary to provide flexibility to industries to ensure that ambition is achievable.'
— Chris Bowen

First Dog on the Moon, *The Guardian*

David Rowe, *Australian Financial Review*

'The Albanese government gets things done. And nowhere is it more important … than in the area of climate policy after 10 years of denial and delay. Today, we're a big step closer to passing the Safeguard Mechanism reforms through the Parliament. We're also, therefore, a big step closer to achieving our targets of net zero and 43 per cent by 2030.'
 — Chris Bowen

'The Greens have huge concerns with other parts of the scheme, such as the rampant use of offsets and the low emissions-reduction targets, but we're prepared to put those concerns aside and give Labor's scheme a chance if Labor agrees to stop opening new coal and gas projects.'
 — Adam Bandt

'Driving all this is the fossil fuel industry. Enabling it are political leaders unwilling to bring this industry under control and who promote policies such as offsetting and massive gas expansion that simply enable this industry to continue.'
 — Bill Hare

Brett Lethbridge, *The Courier Mail*

Jon Kudelka, *The Saturday Paper*

Glen Le Lievre, *Patreon*

'We've secured a pollution trigger that, for the first time in history, means new projects must be assessed for their impact on climate pollution and they can be stopped. Labor now has the power to stop coal and gas projects that would breach the pollution cap. Every new coal and gas project that gets approved from here on in is Labor's direct responsibility.'
— Adam Bandt

'New facilities will be obliged to comply with the world's best practice on emissions.'
— Chris Bowen

'This is a big day for the Greens movement, but an even bigger day for the Traditional Owners and mob whose lands and waters are under threat from the climate bombs that are Barossa and Beetaloo projects. I have stood in solidarity with you, on-Country, and witnessed first hand how these companies and their projects would destroy your way of life.'
— Dorinda Cox

Matt Golding, *The Age*

John Spooner, *The Australian*

David Pope, *The Canberra Times*

'Sitting in Labor ministers' offices having cups of tea and moving commas around is a model for change that is demonstrably failing ... Some groups have had this access for decades and haven't even stopped Labor from taking donations from fossil fuel corporations, let alone convinced it to take real climate action.'
— Nick McKim

'Don't tell us, prime minister, that we're ambulance chasing, the time for that is over. This is the time for reasonable and mature responses to the global science on this, and that's not what we're getting in this pathetic legislation.'
— Bob Brown

'The fight is not over.'
— Adam Bandt

'I can tell you that people are turning to the Greens because they can see they have a genuine response to climate change — not a big-business one. They are not corporate-captured, as Labor and the Coalition are.'
— Bob Brown

First Dog on the Moon, *The Guardian*

John Spooner, *The Australian*

'This Soviet-style policy is a form of nationalisation. This will result in companies needing fiscal-stability agreements with the government before new gas-supply projects can take investment decisions in order to secure capital, just as would be the case if they were operating in Argentina, Venezuela, or Nigeria.'
— Kevin Gallagher, Santos

'Some of those executives might want to hold on to every single dollar of their Putin profits, but we are making what's right in the national economic interest.'
— Ed Husic

'Experts are loudly warning that gas price-fixing will result in 19 years of gas supply being commercially stranded and will increase the risk of blackouts in 2023.'
— Angus Taylor

'These are Australia's resources, we should benefit from it … to set us up for the future.'
— David Pocock

Johannes Leak, *The Australian*

Johannes Leak, *The Australian*

no one left behind

Glen Le Lievre, *Patreon*

'No one is left behind because we should always look after the disadvantaged and the vulnerable. But also no one held back, because we should always support aspiration and opportunity.'
— Anthony Albanese

'To my mum, who's beaming down on us. Thank you. And I hope there are families in public housing watching this tonight. Because I want every parent to be able to tell their child, no matter where you live or where you come from, in Australia the doors of opportunity are open to us all.'
— Anthony Albanese

Jon Kudelka, *The Saturday Paper*

Cathy Wilcox, *The Sydney Morning Herald*

Brett Lethbridge, *The Courier Mail*

'I'm interested in how to make the NDIS as strong and as sustainable as it can be … at no point have I come under any pressure from the treasurer … to slash and burn the NDIS to subsidise something else.'
— Bill Shorten

'Our community was building trust between the federal government and the disability community; instead, this government have chosen to take us back to square one.'
— Jordon Steele-John

'We want to see the scheme sustainable into the future, but we don't want to create fear for the community — people need to be reassured that their supports are safe.'
— People with Disability Australia

'The NDIS isn't paying for subs, as Peter Dutton suggested.'
— Bill Shorten

Dean Alston, *The West Australian*

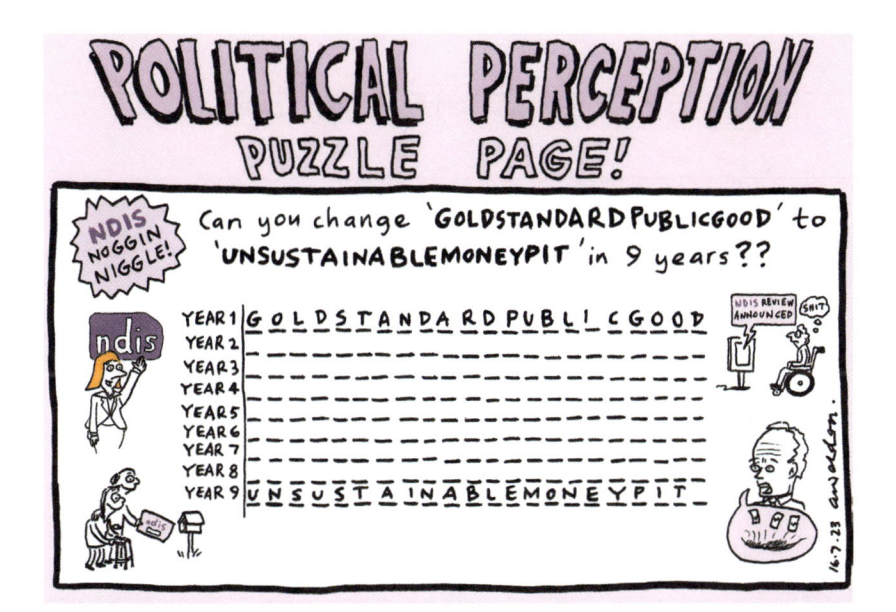

Andrew Weldon, *The Big Issue*

Matt Golding, *The Age*

Jon Kudelka, *The Saturday Paper*

First Dog on the Moon, *The Guardian*

Sean Leahy, *The Courier Mail*

Christopher Downes, *The Mercury*

Mark Knight, *Herald Sun*

Megan Herbert, *The Age*

Glen Le Lievre, *Eureka Street*

'While renters get smashed by record rent increases, and soaring property prices lock millions out of ever owning a home, Labor's dodgy housing plan shows they haven't even started to comprehend the scale of the crisis.'
— Max Chandler-Mather

'Unlimited rent increases should be illegal ... The pressure is now on the prime minister and the Labor premiers to act on a rent freeze and limit rent increases. ... This is a test for Labor. It's wall-to-wall Labor across the mainland, so rent rises are their responsibility.'
— Adam Bandt

'[The Greens] deal in protests, we deal in progress ... They see issues to campaign on; we see challenges to act on. They want to build their profile; we want to build more homes.'
— Anthony Albanese

Dean Alston, *The West Australian*

Cathy Wilcox, *The Sydney Morning Herald*

Jon Kudelka, *The Saturday Paper*

'Housing, to the generation the Greens are talking to, which is mostly people under the age of 45, is just as important as climate change now. And the electoral impacts will be potentially just as profound as they were for climate in 2022.'
— Kos Samaras

'We're not asking for the world. We're asking for a small amount of the budget surplus, $2.5 billion, to go towards public and affordable housing.'
— Max Chandler-Mather

'You have the Coalition, One Nation, and the Greens in the new No-alition, a No-alition saying no to improving housing affordability.'
— Anthony Albanese

'All Labor is offering is a gamble on the stockmarket that may not even build a single home.'
— Max Chandler-Mather

'You're a joke, mate.'
— Anthony Albanese

Sean Leahy, *The Courier Mail*

First Dog on the Moon, *The Guardian*

John Farmer, *The Mercury*

Andrew Weldon, *The Big Issue*

'Our judgment is that we are unlikely to see wages growth consistent with the inflation target before 2024. This is the basis for our assessment that the cash rate is very likely to remain at its current level until at least 2024.'
— Philip Lowe, 2021

'This is the greatest drop in workers' real pay in recorded history — no wonder one in four workers are skipping meals ... The RBA was predicting much higher wage growth, and once again they've got it wrong. Not only is their thinking stuck in the 1970s, they're basing interest rate decisions on flawed projections.'
— Sally McManus

'It's really tough, I understand that. I hear those stories with a very heavy heart. Many have forgotten the really serious damage [untrammelled inflation] does to people, livelihoods, and the functioning of the economy if it persists. It leads to higher interest rates and more unemployment ... People are free to express their opinion, but it is the job of the central bank to control inflation.'
— Philip Lowe

Christopher Downes,
The Mercury

Dean Alston,
The West Australian

Johannes Leak, *The Australian*

'The way that this ends up fixing itself, unfortunately, is through higher housing prices and higher rents ... Because as rents go up people decide not to move out of home, or you don't have that home office, you get a flatmate ... The increase in supply can't happen immediately, but higher prices do lead people to economise on housing. That's the price mechanism at work. We need more people on average to live in each dwelling, and prices do that.'
— Philip Lowe

'I think those who are sitting on that minimum wage, if they're really not happy with their job, should start looking around.'
— Ross McEwan, NAB

'An overemphasis on wages as a driver of persistent inflation, reliance on forecasting and modelling tools that offered limited insights on the supply side of the economy, and the way [that] forward guidance and the yield target had been designed and used all contributed.'
— RBA review

Matt Golding, *The Age*

Mark Knight, *Herald Sun*

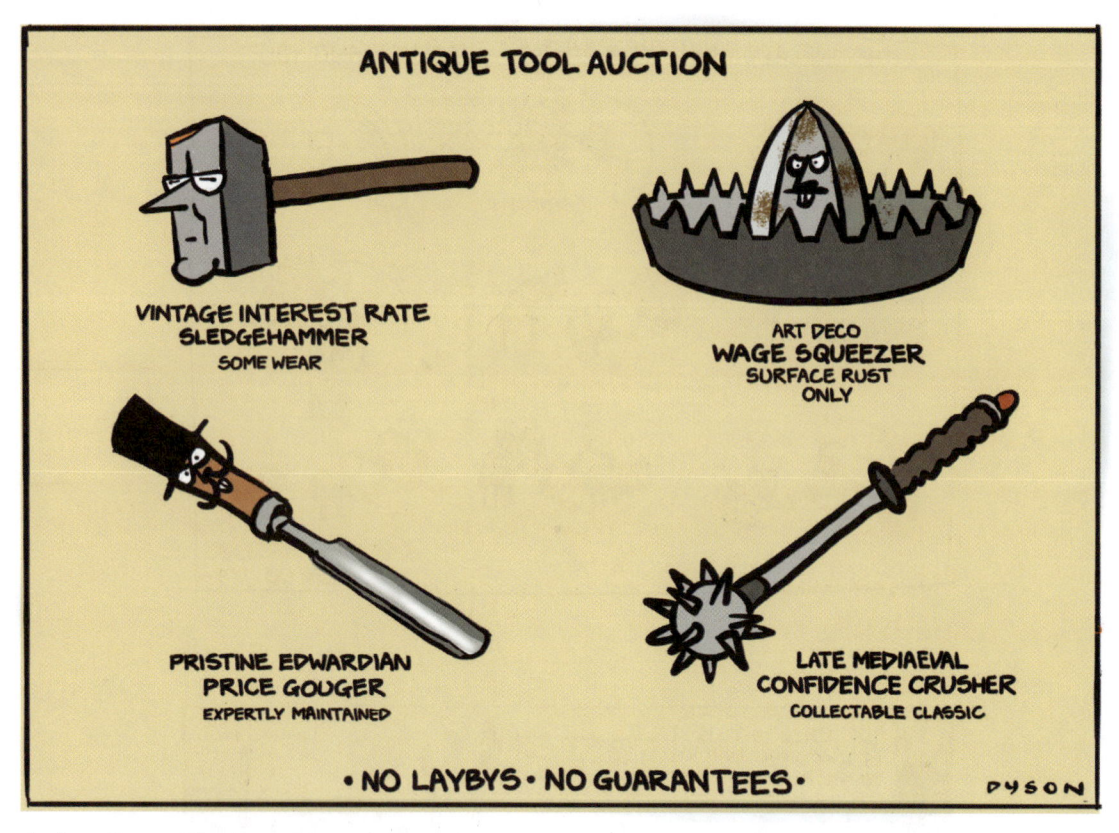

Andrew Dyson, *The Age*

'Fiscal policy most of the time is not as effective at managing inflation ... Except for in extraordinary times, it's not the best tool to use to manage aggregate demand. Interest rates are the more nimble tool. They're a blunt policy tool, but they are nimble.'
— Philip Lowe

'So we should be having a conversation about fiscal measures, like price controls and a super profits tax, but instead we're just letting the RBA belt people over the head with interest rate increases and telling them to exercise wage restraint. It's beyond a joke.'
— Ross Gittins

'The RBA's objectives for monetary policy should be clarified as a dual mandate to contribute to price stability and full employment.'
— RBA review

Brett Lethbridge, *The Courier Mail*

John Farmer, *The Mercury*

THE WAR ON INFLATION

Glen Le Lievre, *Patreon*

'Given the importance of avoiding a prices-wages spiral, the board will continue to pay close attention to both the evolution of labour costs and the price-setting behaviour of firms in the period ahead.'
— Philip Lowe

'There is no evidence of a wage-price spiral in our economy … We don't have an inflation challenge in our economy because wages are too high, but because of a war in Ukraine, pressure on global supply chains, and other challenges in our own economy ignored for too long.'
— Jim Chalmers

'What we've got is an inflationary crisis caused by [corporate] profiteering and supply-chain shocks led by Covid, led by a war in Ukraine — things that the Australian people aren't responsible for.'
— Zach Smith, CFMEU

John Farmer, *The Mercury*

Cathy Wilcox, *The Sydney Morning Herald*

Fiona Katauskas, *The Guardian*

Cathy Wilcox, *The Sydney Morning Herald*

David Pope, *The Canberra Times*

'The board needs members such as former Fair Work Commission president Iain Ross who understand real-world wage-setting systems and the relationship between wages, unemployment, and inflation.'
— Sally McManus

'There is a risk of groupthink that can be driven by concentrated policy and operational decision-making processes and a lack of meaningful conversations with senior leaders about why decisions are taken ... While the RBA has introduced initiatives to encourage staff to speak up, these factors continue to inhibit constructive challenge and debate and stifle innovation and creativity.'
— RBA review

'The diversity must include representation of the interests of people who are the most disadvantaged, outside the labour market, and struggling the most to deal with inflation and unemployment. We also need to see community and human services sector perspectives reflected, recognising that our sector is likely to be one of the major areas of growth in employment and the economy.'
— Cassandra Goldie

David Rowe, *Australian Financial Review*

'Replacing one RBA insider with another is business-as-usual, and a clear signal that renters and mortgage holders will keep getting smashed to solve a problem they didn't cause. Labor needs to tax corporate super profits and wealth. That would be anti-inflationary and reduce the pressure on the RBA to use the only tool it has.'
— Nick McKim

'Political power, its management and employment in office, must, in a working democracy, take precedence over any subordinate bureaucratic structure.'
— Paul Keating

'In the age-old struggle between labour and capital, wages and profits, most economists have decided long ago whose side they're on, and long ago lost sight of how one-eyed they've become.'
— Ross Gittins

Johannes Leak, *The Australian*

Mark Knight, *Herald Sun*

David Rowe, *Australian Financial Review*

'People can see what we're doing here … we're proposing a change that will have an impact on 0.5 per cent of the population.'
  — Jim Chalmers

'Australian super is Australians' money … It is clear that Labor is prepared to break a promise to charge more tax.'
  — Angus Taylor

'A media circus and Liberal Party pearl-clutching for super tax concessions for only the ultra wealthy — but nothing for the victims of Robodebt? C'mon!'
  — Bill Shorten

'Modest changes to superannuation tax concessions to help pay for a $9,000 tax cut is just a money-go-round scheme for the rich.'
  — Nick McKim

Sean Leahy,
The Courier Mail

John Shakespeare,
The Sydney Morning Herald

Fiona Katauskas, *The Echidna*

'If the government is worried about how we'll pay for essential services like Medicare and NDIS in the future, it beggars belief that they're pushing ahead with the stage-three tax cuts.'
— Larissa Waters

'Labor wants to disproportionately focus on and demonise those earning a good income. It's a return to the class war rhetoric we saw in 2019. And if they want to stand around in Sydney, where I'm standing now, and tell people that they earn too much to deserve the tax relief they were promised … they should say that.'
— Sussan Ley

'I think the more honourable course for Labor would be to use the power it now has in government following the election … to promote the interests of the people of Australia … And that means taking steps to repeal stage three and to get on with … building a fairer and healthier and happier country for all its citizens.'
— Bernie Fraser

Matt Golding, *The Age*

Jon Kudelka, *The Saturday Paper*

David Pope, *The Canberra Times*

'This is what values-based capitalism can look like.'
— Jim Chalmers

'Almost a year into their term, and despite a windfall in both political and budget capital, we've seen yet another budget that's a step in the right direction but lacking in ambition.'
— David Pocock

'The biggest broken promise is one the prime minister made before the election … that no one would be held back and no one would be left behind. This is a budget that tells Australians the government knows it's tough, but doesn't have solutions. It's a budget that tells Australians pain is coming, and leaves them on their own to deal with.'
— Angus Taylor

'The fault lines in our housing market have become so deep, and the number of Australians plunging over the financial cliff into homelessness so numerous, that it is time for a fundamental shift, not just incremental change.'
— Homelessness Australia

Dean Alston, *The West Australian*

Brett Lethbridge, *The Courier Mail*

David Rowe, *Australian Financial Review*

'The young boy from Marrickville would have said that this is a budget that looks after people, that makes a positive difference ... taking pressure off families whilst we're not adding to pressure on inflation.'
— Anthony Albanese

'The government has made a political choice to sacrifice the lives of people who are on the lowest incomes for the sake of a budget surplus.'
— The AntiPoverty Centre

'Our job in this budget is to provide responsible cost-of-living relief, targeted to the most vulnerable people in ways that don't add to inflation, at the same time as we show spending restraint in the budget and invest in the drivers of growth, including in areas like the clean-energy transformation.'
— Jim Chalmers

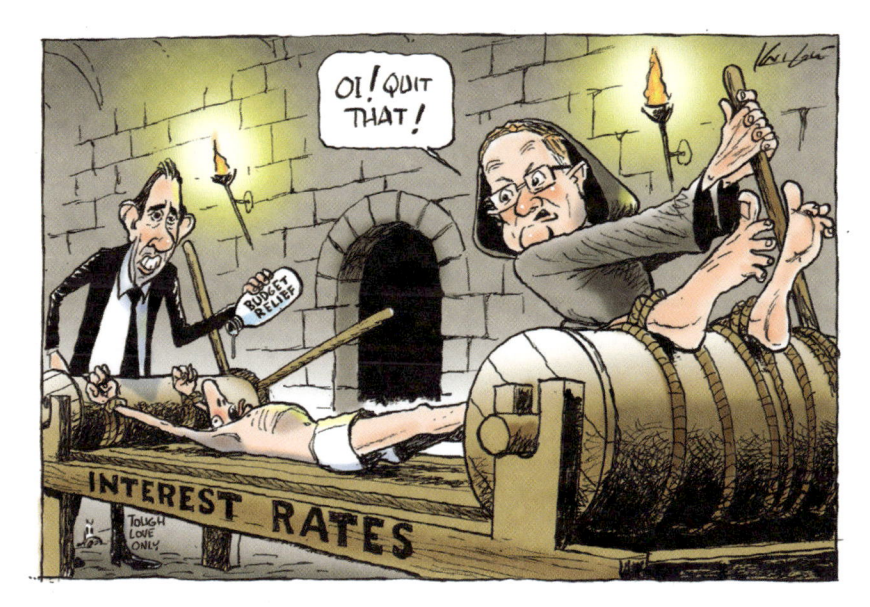

Mark Knight, *Herald Sun*

David Pope, *The Canberra Times*

Matt Golding, *The Age*

'These are the choices of a mature nation … that understands that a bright future calls for more than sunny optimism.'
— Anthony Albanese

'We're not here in Labor for mere gestures. We are here to change the country, to go the distance, to get to the destination, to deliver the better future that we promised.'
— Anthony Albanese

'If you're pro-human rights, you need to be pro-AUKUS. If you're pro-peace, you need to be pro-AUKUS … If you're pro-trying to bring manufacturing back to this country, you need to be pro-AUKUS.'
— Pat Conroy

'Deterrence is not a one-word justification for any and every defence acquisition.'
— Josh Wilson

David Pope, *The Canberra Times*

David Rowe, *Australian Financial Review*

Matt Golding, *The Age*

'The key conclusion is that an ageing population and climate change present significant long-term risks for the economy and the sustainability of government finances. As the population ages, the rate of economic growth will slow. Pressures for government spending will increase, particularly in the health sector. At the same time, we will face the global challenge of climate change, which represents the largest threat to our environment and one of the most significant challenges to our economic sustainability.'
— Intergenerational Report

'There will never be a quiet time to think about the future.'
— Jim Chalmers

'They're not thinking about 40 years from now … They're thinking about 40 days from now.'
— Angus Taylor

Alan Moir,
The Sydney Morning Herald

John Shakespeare,
The Sydney Morning Herald

back by popular demand

David Pope, *The Canberra Times*

'AUKUS gets Australia off the fence. We have them locked in now for the next 40 years.'
— Kurt Campbell

'I made it clear to US President George Bush … that Labor remained a firm supporter of the ANZUS alliance, but that the true test and strength of any alliance was the ability to tell good and trusted friends when they were wrong. That was such a time, and history has confirmed it. We can't reverse history, but we must learn from it.'
— Simon Crean, 2018

'The illegal we do immediately; the unconstitutional takes a little longer.'
— Henry Kissinger

Cathy Wilcox, *The Sydney Morning Herald*

Dean Alston, *The West Australian*

Glen Le Lievre, *Patreon*

'Ben Roberts-Smith is innocent and … scumbag journalists should be held to account. And quote me on that.'
 — Kerry Stokes

'For such a long time in Afghanistan we have had a culture of impunity. For decades … governments, armies, warring parties have killed Afghan civilians … and have gotten away with it … The message, continuously to Afghans, is that your life does not have value and the harm that comes to you, you just have to live with it.'
 — Shaharzad Akbar

'It doesn't count as a war crime if you had fun.'
 — Russian bar-room graffiti, Ukraine

'I'm pretty sure in other countries at the moment, they're not having woke morning teas. They're getting on with how they can protect and defend our country.'
 — Peter Dutton

Sean Leahy, *The Courier Mail*

Jon Kudelka, *The Saturday Paper*

Cathy Wilcox, *The Sydney Morning Herald*

'Ministers and command knew what was happening, but looked away, and even if they didn't know, the reality is chain of command is responsible.'
 — David McBride

'This case provides further impetus, if it was needed, for the attorney-general to step in and end the unjust prosecution of Afghanistan war crimes whistleblower David McBride.'
 — David Shoebridge

'I now realise that what I was coming up against was more than the horrific acts of a few rogue soldiers. It was the cult of brand SAS, the cult of the male warrior.'
 — Samantha Crompvoets

'There is a culture of cover-up at the highest levels of the Australian Defence Force. It is the ultimate boys' club.'
 — Jacqui Lambie

John Kudelka, *The Saturday Paper*

First Dog on the Moon, *The Guardian*

Mark David, *independentaustralia.net*

135

David Rowe, *Australian Financial Review*

'When Australia looks north, we don't see a void for others to impose their will. We see a community of nations whose actions and decisions are essential to building prosperity and preserving peace in the Indo-Pacific.'
— Anthony Albanese

'The United States and Taiwan should lay plans for a targeted scorched-earth strategy that would render Taiwan not just unattractive if ever seized by force, but positively costly to maintain.'
— *Parameters*, US Army War College journal

'Every Labor Party branch member will wince when they realise that the party we all fight for is returning to our former colonial master, Britain, to find our security in Asia — 236 years after Europeans first grabbed the continent from its Indigenous people.'
— Paul Keating

Alan Moir, www.moir.com.au

Alan Moir, www.moir.com.au

David Rowe, *Australian Financial Review*

'It ties our fate more closely to the mistaken view that we can always rely on the United States … Mistaken, not because the US is unreliable or feckless, not because the alliance is no longer central to our security, not even because Donald Trump or his ilk might return to the White House. It is mistaken because countries always act in their own interests, and great powers even more so … To anchor policy on any other assumption is to ignore history.'
— Peter Varghese

'This reckless alliance, cooked up by the Morrison government and backed by Labor, fundamentally compromises Australia's sovereignty by aligning us with the military and nuclear strategies of the world's biggest powers.'
— David Shoebridge

'To be an enemy of America can be dangerous, but to be a friend is fatal.'
— Henry Kissinger

Cathy Wilcox, *The Sydney Morning Herald*

David Pope, *The Canberra Times*

Mark Knight, *Herald Sun*

'We must build the People's Liberation Army into a great wall of steel that effectively safeguards national sovereignty, security, and development interests.'
— Xi Jinping

'When submarines are provided from the United States to Australia, it's not like they're lost. They will just be deployed by the closest possible allied force.'
— Kurt Campbell

'The "threat" from China's increased military capabilities is said to be its assertion of sovereignty over the South China Sea. How is it an existential threat to Australia's sovereignty, and why are we gambling our future on a US-led war there?'
— David Shoebridge

Badiucao, *@badiucao*

Cathy Wilcox, *The Sydney Morning Herald*

Alan Moir, *www.moir.com.au*

John Farmer, *The Mercury*

David Rowe, *Australian Financial Review*

'This is a $368 billion nuclear-powered raid on public education, health, housing, and First Nations justice that will starve core services for decades to come.'
— David Shoebridge

'This AUKUS program has been orchestrated in total secrecy … a fait accompli without any debate or resistance … There are some things that should properly be kept secret around a submarine, but these things should not include nuclear stewardship, nuclear regulation, nuclear safety, or how to deal with operational waste and spent fuel.'
— Rex Patrick

'I think what's really been missing in this is a proper full-scale debate about its implications … what it means for Australia and our place in the world, our relationships with China, and our relationships with the region.'
— Ben Oquist

David Pope,
The Canberra Times

Matt Golding,
The Age

Glen Le Lievre, *Eureka Street*

Andrew Weldon, *The Big Issue*

Alan Moir, www.moir.com.au

'Ratifying an undertaking of this magnitude should have been subject to thorough scrutiny and debate through all levels of the Australian Labor party, and in the public realm. Instead, the original announcement, made in secret by three national leaders, two of whom have already left office, has now been given effect by a Labor government.'
— Peter Garrett

'The sheer size of the decision to share this capability with Australia … puts all three countries in a position where it's too big for it to fail on the part of any of those countries.'
— Richard Marles

'Has Defence ever delivered a major construction or weapons-delivery program on time and on budget?'
— Peter Garrett

'Future technologies will make the oceans broadly transparent, and counter-detection technologies will not have the same salience in the decades ahead as they have had previously.'
— *Transparent Oceans*, National Security College

Andrew Dyson, *The Age*

Andrew Dyson, *The Age*

David Rowe, *Australian Financial Review*

'This week, Anthony Albanese screwed into place the last shackle in the long chain the United States has laid out to contain China.'
    — Paul Keating

'Keating has his views, but in substance and in tone they belong to another time.'
    — Penny Wong

'Of all things, a contemporary Labor government is shunning security in Asia for security in and within the Anglosphere.'
    — Paul Keating

'I don't think that does anything other than diminish him, frankly. But that's a decision that he's made.'
    — Anthony Albanese

David Pope, *The Canberra Times*

Dean Alston, *The West Australian*

Matt Golding, *The Age*

'America has often been talked of as the indispensable power. It remains so. But the nature of that indispensability has changed. As we seek a strategic equilibrium, with all countries exercising their agency to achieve peace and prosperity, America is central to balancing a multipolar region.'
— Penny Wong

'Running around the Pacific Islands with a lei around your neck handing out money, which is what Penny does, is not foreign policy. It's a consular task. Foreign policy is what you do with the great powers: what you do with China, what you do with the United States. This government, the Albanese government, does not employ foreign policy.'
— Paul Keating

'Australia and China have very different political systems and have very different values. It is China that has seen the fastest and most significant growth in military expenditure in the postwar period of any nation, and that is just a fact.'
— Anthony Albanese

David Pope, *The Canberra Times*

Andrew Dyson, *The Age*

David Rowe, *Australian Financial Review*

'China is not a threat — was not a threat, is not a threat, is not going to be a threat in the future — to Australia.'
— Xiao Qian

'Our position on China has been to engage constructively, but … the impediments to trade should be removed.'
— Anthony Albanese

'China is a world trading state — it is not about upending the international system.'
— Paul Keating

'I don't think this will be a big bang and that everything's going to be resolved overnight … The problems didn't occur overnight; they won't be resolved overnight.'
— Don Farrell

Mark Knight, *Herald Sun*

Peter Broelman, *The Echidna*

Badiucao, *@badiucao*

'We disagree with China [on] its attitude towards human rights, we disagree with some of its actions in the South China Sea, we disagree with its much more forward-leaning position in our region, and will stand up for Australian values, will stand up for our national interest.'
— Anthony Albanese

'What if the Chinese said, "What about deaths in custody of Aboriginal people in your prison system?" Wouldn't that be a valid point for them?'
— Paul Keating

'He may have his views, but the government has ours, and we've raised our concerns about the treatment of Uyghurs with the PRC, with China, at all levels.'
— Penny Wong

John Spooner, *The Australian*

Badiucao, *@badiucao*

Glen Le Lievre, *Australian Financial Review*

Glen Le Lievre, *Australian Financial Review*

David Rowe, *Australian Financial Review*

'Order has been restored in Hong Kong, marking a turn for the better in the region … The Taiwan issue is China's own problem to solve.'
  — Xi Jinping

'The wheels of history are rolling on towards reunification and the rejuvenation of the great Chinese nation … We will continue to strive for peaceful reunification with the greatest sincerity and utmost effort, but we will never promise to renounce the use of force.'
  — Xi Jinping

'Western countries led by the United States have contained and suppressed us in an all-round way, which has brought unprecedented severe challenges to our development.'
  — Xi Jinping

David Rowe, *Australian Financial Review*

'China … is watching to see the price Russia pays, or the reward it receives, for its aggression in Ukraine … South Korea and Japan were clearly concerned that what was happening in Europe today could happen in Asia tomorrow.'
  — Jens Stoltenberg, NATO

'The question Europeans need to answer … is it in our interest to accelerate a crisis on Taiwan? No. The worse thing would be to think that we Europeans must become followers on this topic and take our cue from the US agenda and a Chinese overreaction.'
  — Emmanuel Macron

'Macron is doing the world a service putting a spike into Stoltenberg's wheel — reminding all of us that NATO is a military organisation, not a civil one, and an organisation focused on Europe and the Atlantic.'
  — Paul Keating

Badiucao, *The Age*

Andrew Dyson, *The Age*

David Rowe, *Australian Financial Review*

'Change is coming that hasn't happened in 100 years. And we are driving this change together.'
 — Xi Jinping

'It looks they have forgotten the consequences of the Nazi striving for world domination. They have forgotten who destroyed that monster, that absolute evil, who it was who stood up to … liberate the peoples of Europe.'
 — Vladimir Putin

'A dictatorship, by its very nature, cannot exist without enemies, which means war.'
 — Mikhail Shishkin

'His mistake was going in. He would've never gone in if I was president. We used to talk about it, too.'
 — Donald Trump

Peter Broelman, *www.broelman.com.au*

Badiucao, *@badiucao*

Glen Le Lievre, *Australian Financial Review*

'The Western globalist elite are still asserting their exceptionalism … provoking bloody conflicts and coups, sowing hatred, Russophobia, and aggressive nationalism … destroying traditional family values that make a human a human.'
   — Vladimir Putin

'We pray to the Lord that he bring the madmen to reason and help them understand that any desire to destroy Russia will mean the end of the world.'
   — Patriarch Kirill, Russian Orthodox Church

'When a war will be called a war, and a usurper a usurper; and when those who kindled and unleashed this war, rather than those who tried to stop it, will be recognised as criminals … our society will open its eyes and be horrified by what terrible crimes were committed on its behalf, and the long, difficult but vital path toward the recovery and restoration of Russia, its return to the community of civilised countries, will begin.'
   — Vladimir Kara-Murza, Russian opposition

Alan Moir, *www.moir.com.au*

Alan Moir, *www.moir.com.au*

David Rowe, *Australian Financial Review*

'The collective West is essentially waging an undeclared war against our countries.'
— Sergei Shoigu

'The war was needed ... so that Shoigu could become a marshal ... so that he could get a second Hero of Russia medal. The war wasn't needed to demilitarise or denazify Ukraine.'
— Yevgeny V. Prigozhin

'What we're seeing is a stab in the back.'
— Vladimir Putin

'Congratulations on the Victory Day achieved by our grandfathers. But it's a big question what we're celebrating. We just need to remember them, and that's it. And not fuck around on Red Square.'
— Yevgeny V. Prigozhin

Cathy Wilcox, *The Sydney Morning Herald*

John Spooner, *The Australian*

Cathy Wilcox, *The Sydney Morning Herald*

'World War III has never been closer than it is right now … I will clean house of all of the warmongers and America-Last globalists in the Deep State, the Pentagon, the State Department, and the national security industrial complex.'
— Donald Trump

'I don't think it's in our interest to be getting into a proxy war with China, getting involved over things like the Borderlands or over Crimea.'
— Ron DeSantis

'The Russians are dying … it's the best money we've ever spent.'
— Lindsey Graham

'The pumping in of weapons can continue … Our enemies are doing just that, not wanting to understand that their goals will certainly lead to … loss for everyone. A collapse. Apocalypse.'
— Dmitry Medvedev

Glen Le Lievre, *Australian Financial Review*

Sean Leahy, *The Courier Mail*

David Pope, *The Canberra Times*

'The last time I saw someone on this stage was Bruce Springsteen, and he did not get the welcome that Prime Minister Modi has got. Prime Minister Modi is the boss.'
— Anthony Albanese

'Friends, the scope of India–Australia ties is not limited to merely our two countries. It is also linked to regional stability, peace, and global welfare.'
— Narendra Modi

'The history of India is being painted as a black-and-white narrative of Hindus versus Muslims. But it was never so.'
— Syed Ali Nadeem Rezavi

'The Australian government should not repeat the same mistakes it made with the Chinese government by pursuing deeper trade engagement while sidelining human rights concerns.'
— Human Rights Watch

Andrew Dyson, *The Age*

Andrew Dyson, *The Age*

David Rowe, *Australian Financial Review*

'We are clarifying that the West Bank, including East Jerusalem, and Gaza were occupied by Israel following the 1967 war and that the occupation continues.'
— Penny Wong

'Labor's backroom decisions on Israel and the Palestinian territories have everything to do with managing factional differences … and nothing to do with advancing a lasting two-state outcome.'
— Simon Birmingham

'The Jewish people have an exclusive and unquestionable right to all areas of the land of Israel.'
— Benjamin Netanyahu

'Theres no such thing as Palestinians because there's no such thing as the Palestinian people.'
— Bezalel Smotrich

Cathy Wilcox, *The Sydney Morning Herald*

David Pope, *The Canberra Times*

Cathy Wilcox, *The Sydney Morning Herald*

'So many dozens of kids didn't die so a year later we will go back to how we were before September 2022 … Whether or not the regime wants to accept, we will hit the streets again and there's no going back. We are already planning huge protests leading up to the one-year anniversary of Mahsa's death. There will be more arrests or worse.'
— Tehran student, anon

'When we get our bodies back, we will get our country back.'
— Iranian woman, anon

'Put aside all wickedness. Today is the last day of the riots. Do not come to the streets anymore.'
— Iranian Revolutionary Guard

'We are not the same women the Taliban suppressed 20 years ago. We have changed and they will have to accept it, even if we have to give up our lives for it.'
— Afghan woman, anon

Alan Moir, *www.moir.com.au*

David Pope, *The Canberra Times*

Alan Moir, *www.moir.com.au*

Matt Bissett-Johnson, *Melbourne Observer*

Cathy Wilcox, *The Sydney Morning Herald*

'The Murdochs and their slew of poisonous Fox News commentators are the unindicted co-conspirators of this continuing crisis.'
— Bernard Keane

'Getting creamed by CNN! Guess our viewers don't want to watch it. Hard enough for me!'
— Rupert Murdoch

'Fox knew the truth … It knew the allegations against Dominion were "outlandish" and "crazy" and "ludicrous" and "nuts". Yet it used the power and influence of its platform to promote that false story.'
— Dominion court papers

'This settlement reflects Fox's continued commitment to the highest journalistic standards.'
— Fox News

Christopher Downes, *The Mercury*

John Spooner, *The Australian*

Cathy Wilcox, *The Sydney Morning Herald*

Prosecutor: 'It's true you can grab them by the pussy?'
Trump: 'Well, if you look over the last million years, I guess that's been largely true. Not always, but largely true. Unfortunately or fortunately.'

'I WILL APPOINT A REAL SPECIAL "PROSECUTOR" TO GO AFTER THE MOST CORRUPT PRESIDENT IN THE HISTORY OF THE USA, JOE BIDEN, THE ENTIRE BIDEN CRIME FAMILY, & ALL OTHERS INVOLVED WITH THE DESTRUCTION OF OUR ELECTIONS, BORDERS, & COUNTRY ITSELF!'
  — Donald Trump

'The notion that a politician making efforts to hide unflattering information from the American voter constitutes a criminal offense sounds a lot to me like criminalising politics.'
  — Thomas Kenniff

Matt Golding, *The Age*

'If you want to get to President Trump, you are going to have go through me, and you are going to have to go through 75 million Americans just like me. And I'm going to tell you, most of us are card-carrying members of the NRA. That's not a threat, that's a public service announcement.'
— Kari Lake

'These un-American witch hunts will fail and President Trump will be re-elected to the White House so he can save our Country from the abuse, incompetence, and corruption that is running through the veins of our Country at levels never seen before.'
— Donald Trump

'This is a communist country. We've been taken over. It's not the America that we all thought that we all had. We're not a free country anymore.'
— Marjorie Taylor Greene

Warren Brown, *The Daily Telegraph*

Andrew Dyson, *The Age*

David Rowe, *Australian Financial Review*

'Each of these conspiracies — which built on the widespread mistrust the defendant was creating through pervasive and destabilising lies about election fraud — targeted a bedrock function of the United States federal government: the nation's process of collecting, counting, and certifying the results of the presidential election.'
— Trump's indictment

'The third indictment ... illustrates in shocking detail that the violence of that day was the culmination of a months-long criminal plot led by the former president to defy democracy and overturn the will of the American people.'
— Chuck Schumer

'IF YOU GO AFTER ME, I'M COMING AFTER YOU.'
— Donald Trump

Alan Moir, *www.moir.com.au*

Matt Golding, *The Age*

David Pope, *The Canberra Times*

'I call upon all persons of goodwill in The United Kingdom of Great Britain and Northern Ireland, and of the other Realms and the Territories, to make their homage, in heart and voice, to their undoubted King, defender of all.'
— Archbishop of Canterbury

'I believe as Australian prime minister, I have a particular responsibility to represent the nation in a way that respects the constitutional arrangements which are there, and I certainly will undertake that.'
— Anthony Albanese

'Dare not think about this too much. Because then this illusion shatters. We would have to think of the coronation regalia and the crown of stolen jewels. The stolen land. The genocide. The brutality. I would think about the declaration of martial law on my people, the Wiradjuri — 200 years ago next year — in the name of the Crown.'
— Stan Grant

'The historic and momentous occasion of the crowning of Australia's king was not an opportunity for elements within the ABC to pursue their pet topics and tortured view of history without even trying to provide a semblance of balance.'
— Eric Abetz

First Dog on the Moon, *The Guardian*

Reg Lynch, *The Sun-Herald*

'Will you to the utmost of your power maintain the laws of God, the true profession of the Gospel, and the Protestant reformed religion established by law? And will you maintain and preserve inviolably the settlement of the Church of England, and the doctrine, worship, discipline, and government thereof, as by law established in England?'
— King's Coronation Oath

'The great irony is … we're experiencing national angst and psychological trauma in trying to deal with the complexity of our history, and almost the entirety of that history that we're yet to reconcile was created by the Crown.'
— Craig Foster

'Listen. Strange women lying in ponds distributing swords is no basis for a system of government. Supreme executive power derives from a mandate from the masses, not from some farcical aquatic ceremony.'
— Monty Python

'If you ever want an illustration of why Australia should become a republic, it's a frothing and possibly pickled member of the MCC targeting Usman Khawaja in the Long Room at Lords.'
— Matt Thistelwaite

Mark Knight, *Herald Sun*

Dean Alston, *The West Australian*

David Rowe

This year we lost Bruce Petty, a true legend of Australian political cartooning.

A brilliant cartoonist, artist, and filmmaker, Bruce, more importantly, was a wonderfully generous and inspiring human being.

Bruce had an ability to capture personalities with a casual scribble, or so it seemed, but caricature wasn't really his thing. He was primarily driven by ideas, and was in constant pursuit of the deep structures and hidden workings at the intersections of finance and power, often through crazy, complicated conceptual maps. His work was always guided by a profound moral sensibility and desire for justice.

Bruce was a major presence in every edition of *Best Australian Political Cartoons* until 2016, when he retired from editorial cartooning. There has been a huge Petty-shaped hole in it since.

We loved you, Bruce.

Thanks for everything.